Success With

Multiplication & Division

■ SCHOLASTIC

Editor: Ourania Papacharalambous
Cover design by Tannaz Fassihi; cover illustration by Kevin Zimmer
Interior design by Mina Chen
Interior illustrations by Carol Tiernon; Doug Jones (4, 6, 15, 20, 31–33, 42); Mike Moran (14)
All other images @ Shutterstock.com

ISBN 978-1-338-79854-8
Scholastic Inc., 557 Broadway, New York, NY 10012
Copyright © 2022 Scholastic Inc.
All rights reserved. Printed in the U.S.A.
First printing, January 2022
1 2 3 4 5 6 7 8 9 10   40 29 28 27 26 25 24 23 22

INTRODUCTION

Parents and teachers alike will find *Scholastic Success With Multiplication & Division* to be a valuable resource. Students will enjoy completing a wide variety of engaging activities as they sharpen their skills with multiplication and division. On page 4, you will find a list of the key skills covered in the activities throughout this book. Remember to praise students for their efforts and successes!

TABLE OF CONTENTS

Grade-Appropriate Skills Covered in *Scholastic Success With Multiplication & Division: Grade 3*

Interpret products of whole numbers, e.g., interpret 5 × 7 as the total number of objects in 5 groups of 7 objects each.

Interpret whole-number quotients of whole numbers, e.g., interpret 56 ÷ 8 as the number of objects in each share when 56 objects are partitioned equally into 8 shares, or as a number of shares when 56 objects are partitioned into equal shares of 8 objects each.

Use multiplication and division within 100 to solve word problems in situations involving equal groups, arrays, and measurement quantities.

Determine the unknown whole number in a multiplication or division equation relating three whole numbers.

Apply properties of operations as strategies to multiply and divide.

Understand division as an unknown-factor problem.

Fluently multiply and divide within 100, using strategies such as the relationship between multiplication and division or properties of operations.

Multiply one-digit whole numbers by multiples of 10 in the range 10-90 using strategies based on place value and properties of operations.

Hopping Along

A **number line** can be used to help you multiply. One factor tells you how long each jump should be. This is like skip-counting. The other factor tells you how many jumps to take.

$2 \times 6 = 12$

x 2 | 0 2 4 6 8 10 12 14 16 18 20 22 24 26 28 30

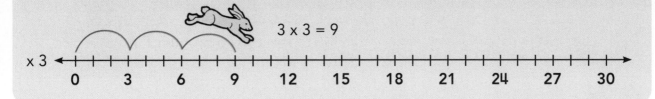

$3 \times 3 = 9$

x 3 | 0 3 6 9 12 15 18 21 24 27 30

Use the number lines above to help you multiply by 2s and 3s.

1. $2 \times 2 = \underline{\hspace{1cm}}$ $3 \times 3 = \underline{\hspace{1cm}}$ $6 \times 2 = \underline{\hspace{1cm}}$

2. $4 \times 3 = \underline{\hspace{1cm}}$ $9 \times 2 = \underline{\hspace{1cm}}$ $7 \times 3 = \underline{\hspace{1cm}}$

3. $7 \times 2 = \underline{\hspace{1cm}}$ $6 \times 3 = \underline{\hspace{1cm}}$ $5 \times 2 = \underline{\hspace{1cm}}$

When multiplying by 0, the product is always 0. When multiplying by 1, the product is always the other factor.

1.

1	8	2	0	3	2
x 2	x 3	x 5	x 3	x 2	x 7

2.

4	3	1	6	0	3
x 2	x 3	x 3	x 2	x 2	x 1

Picture Perfect

An **array** shows a multiplication sentence. The first factor tells how many rows there are. The second factor tells how many are in each row. Here is an array for the multiplication sentence 4 x 4 = 16.

$$
\begin{array}{r}
4 \text{ rows} \\
\times \quad 4 \text{ rows} \\
\hline
16 \text{ in all}
\end{array}
$$

Solve each problem by creating an array.

1 3 x 4 =	**2** 6 x 5 =
3 2 x 5 =	**4** 6 x 4 =
5 8 x 4 =	**6** 3 x 5 =

Shining Brightly

Multiply. Then, write the letter of the problem that matches each product below to learn the names of two of the brightest stars.

B   3
    x 4

R   1
    x 4

A   2
    x 4

F   8
    x 4

P   7
    x 4

S   6
    x 5

U   3
    x 5

E   1
    x 5

U   4
    x 4

I   5
    x 5

G   0
    x 5

S   2
    x 5

O 4 x 5 = _____

D 9 x 5 = _____

I 9 x 4 = _____

N 6 x 4 = _____

S 7 x 5 = _____

C 5 x 8 = _____

Two of the brightest stars are

____ ____ ____ ____ ____ ____ **and** ____ ____ ____ ____ ____ ____ ____ .
 10   25   4   36   16   30   40   8   24   20   28   15   35

A Wheel of Facts

Multiply each number in the center by the numbers on the tire. Write your answers inside the wheel.

 The bike team has 4 members. Each biker rides 9 miles every day. How many miles does the team ride every day altogether? Show your work on another sheet of paper.

Product Drop

Multiply.

$$4 \times 6$$

$$5 \times 2 = \underline{\hspace{1cm}}$$

$$2 \times 6$$

$$3 \times 7$$

$$7 \times 3$$

$$7 \times 1$$

$$6 \times 8 = \underline{\hspace{1cm}}$$

$$6 \times 5$$

$$3 \times 6$$

$$5 \times 6$$

$$3 \times 7$$

$$7 \times 5 = \underline{\hspace{1cm}}$$

$$6 \times 6 = \underline{\hspace{1cm}}$$

$$9 \times 7$$

$$6 \times 7$$

$$6 \times 4$$

$$3 \times 7$$

$$7 \times 7$$

$$7 \times 9$$

$$9 \times 6 = \underline{\hspace{1cm}}$$

$$8 \times 6$$

$$7 \times 6$$

$$8 \times 7 = \underline{\hspace{1cm}}$$

$$5 \times 6 = \underline{\hspace{1cm}}$$

$$7 \times 4 = \underline{\hspace{1cm}}$$

Color the picture above by using the following product code.

0–10 = purple	21–30 = blue	41–50 = yellow	61–70 = pink
11–20 = orange	31–40 = red	51–60 = green	

Scholastic Success With Multiplication & Division • Grade 3   **9**

Sweet Success

Multiply.

1 6 x 6 = _____   2 x 7 = _____

2 1 x 7 = _____   5 x 6 = _____

3 2 x 6 = _____   4 x 7 = _____

4 0 x 7 = _____   7 x 7 = _____

5
```
    6        2        9        4        6        3
  x 7      x 6      x 7      x 6      x 6      x 7
```

6
```
    3        8        1        5        9        7
  x 6      x 7      x 6      x 7      x 6      x 6
```

Ashley bought 4 flowers to plant in each pot. She has 7 pots. How many flowers did she buy in all? Draw a model to solve the problem on another sheet of paper. Then, write a number sentence.

The Product Trail

Multiply to get the lion back to its little cub.

9 x 8 = _____

8 x 5 = _____

9
x 2
___

9 x 4 = _____

3 x 8 = _____

6
x 8
___

8 x 1 = _____

9 x 9 = _____

8 x 4 = _____

8
x 7
___

9 x 3 = _____

8 x 8 = _____

6 x 9 = _____

8
x 2
___

9 x 0 = _____

5 x 9 = _____

There are 8 lions in the jungle. Each has 2 cubs. How many cubs are there altogether? _____

Climbing to the Top

Multiply.

```
    9        8        8        8
  x 6      x 9      x 5      x 6
```

2
```
    9        9        7        2
  x 3      x 9      x 8      x 9
```

3
```
    9        9        2        8        6        8
  x 8      x 0      x 8      x 8      x 9      x 3
```

4
```
    9        9        1        8        0        4
  x 4      x 7      x 9      x 4      x 8      x 8
```

5
```
    3        5        7        1        5        6
  x 9      x 8      x 9      x 8      x 9      x 8
```

The Number Man

Multiply two factors in the triangles. Write each product in the circle between the two factors.

 On another sheet of paper, write two word problems about the Number Man using the multiplication facts 4 x 4 and 7 x 3.

The Case of the Missing Factors

Complete the multiplication chart.

x	0	1	2	3	4	5	6	7	8	9
0				0						
1										
2		2								
3										
4										
5										
6										
7								49		
8										
9										

Use the chart to help the detective find each missing factor.

1. 4 x _____ = 12   7 x _____ = 14   3 x _____ = 27

2. 5 x _____ = 30   6 x _____ = 36   8 x _____ = 64

3. _____ x 4 = 36   _____ x 3 = 24   _____ x 9 = 18

4. _____ x 8 = 56   _____ x 9 = 81   _____ x 1 = 6

5. 9 x _____ = 45   _____ x 9 = 63   3 x _____ = 24

Triple Hit

Multiply around the bases. Start at first base on each baseball field. Then, multiply the number on each base in order. Write each product on home plate.

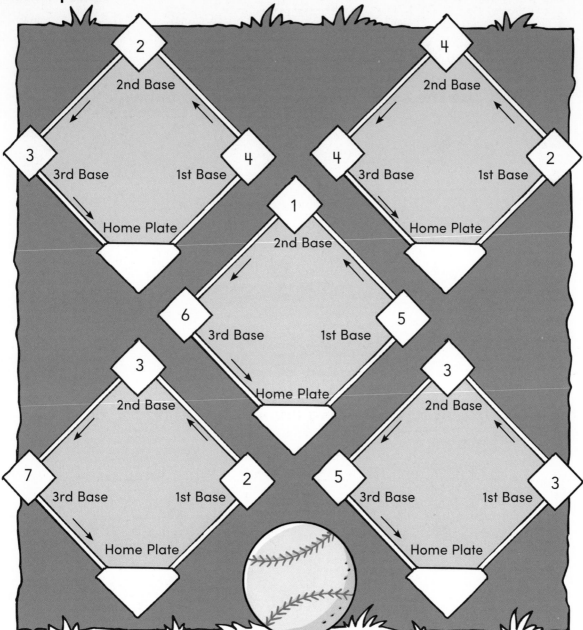

 Four players each have 2 boxes of balls. There are 4 balls in each box. How many balls do the players have altogether? Show your work on another sheet of paper.

One Step, Two Step

To multiply a two-digit number by a one-digit number, follow these steps.

1. Multiply the ones digit.

$4 \times 2 = 8$

```
  34
x  2
____
   8
```

2. Multiply the tens digit.

$3 \times 2 = 6$

```
  34
x  2
____
  68
```

Multiply. Then, use the code to answer the riddle below.

U
```
  23
x  2
```

A
```
  12
x  3
```

Q
```
  14
x  2
```

E
```
  31
x  3
```

E
```
  33
x  3
```

J
```
  71
x  3
```

D
```
  83
x  2
```

!
```
  22
x  4
```

C
```
  24
x  2
```

N
```
  11
x  5
```

R
```
  52
x  4
```

S
```
  33
x  2
```

A
```
  43
x  3
```

S
```
  74
x  2
```

What kind of dancers are math teachers?

| ___ | ___ | ___ | ___ | ___ | ___ | | ___ | ___ | ___ | ___ | ___ | ___ | ___ | ___ |
| 66 | 28 | 46 | 129 | 208 | 99 | | 166 | 36 | 55 | 48 | 93 | 208 | 148 | 88 |

Times Race

Multiply. Time yourself to see how fast you can finish the race.

Three race cars raced around the track. Each race car completed 32 laps. How many laps in all did the race cars complete? Solve the problem on another sheet of paper.

Carry Carefully

Sometimes regrouping will be needed when multiplying with a two-digit number. Follow these steps to solve the problem.

1. Multiply the ones. Regroup if needed.

$7 \times 6 = 42$

$$\begin{array}{r} {}^{4} \\ 47 \\ \times\ \ 6 \\ \hline 2 \end{array}$$

2. Multiply the tens. Add the extra tens.

$4 \times 6 = 24$

$24 + 4 = 28$

$$\begin{array}{r} {}^{4} \\ 47 \\ \times\ \ 6 \\ \hline 282 \end{array}$$

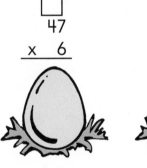

Multiply. Remember to regroup.

1.
☐
36
x 4

☐
25
x 5

☐
63
x 7

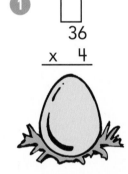

2.
☐
83
x 8

☐
72
x 6

☐
29
x 4

☐
47
x 6

☐
55
x 7

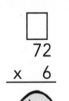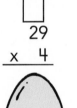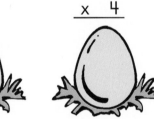

3.
☐
62
x 5

☐
96
x 2

☐
58
x 5

☐
49
x 3

☐
96
x 4

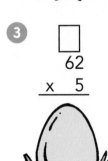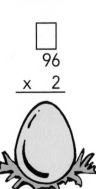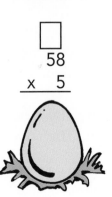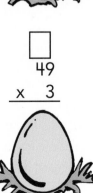

Falling for Multiplication

Multiply. Regroup inside each leaf. Then, use the code
to answer the riddle below.

N 34
x 6

C 17
x 3

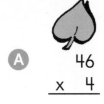

A 46
x 4

H 62
x 5

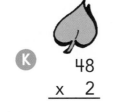

I 53
x 6

B 72
x 7

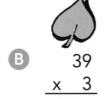

S 28
x 4

K 48
x 2

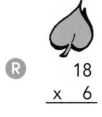

R 18
x 6

B 39
x 3

Where does a tree keep its money?

___ ___   ___ ___ ___ ___ ___ ___   ___ ___ ___ ___ ___!
318 204   117 108 184 204 51 310   504 184 204 96 112

Let's Review!

Multiply. Remember to regroup if needed.

1
53	63	46	73
x 3	x 2	x 4	x 4

2
34	82	35	27
x 6	x 4	x 5	x 4

3
75	23	52	32
x 2	x 7	x 3	x 2

4
29	38	48	84
x 2	x 5	x 6	x 2

Circle each problem above that did not need regrouping. Is there a pattern?

Long Ago...

In the 1970s and 1980s, treats were a lot less expensive. Look at what some things used to cost below. Use these prices to write a multiplication sentence for each problem.

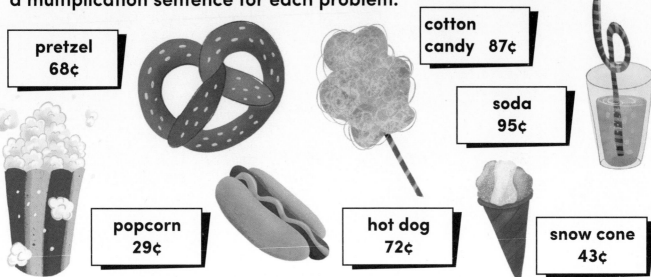

cotton candy   87¢

pretzel 68¢

soda 95¢

popcorn 29¢

hot dog 72¢

snow cone 43¢

---

1 What is the cost of 4 hot dogs?

_____ x _____ = $ _____

2 How much will 6 popcorn bags cost?

_____ x _____ = $ _____

---

3 If you buy 3 pretzels, how much will you spend?

_____ x _____ = $ _____

4 What is the cost of 3 cotton candies?

_____ x _____ = $ _____

---

5 What is the cost of 2 snow cones and 2 popcorns?

_____ x _____ = $ _____

_____ x _____ = $ _____

_____ + _____ = $ _____

6 You bought 3 sodas and 2 pretzels. How much did you spend?

_____ x _____ = $ _____

_____ x _____ = $ _____

_____ + _____ = $ _____

Sweet and Juicy

Multiply. Color an apple if you find its product.

1
$$203 \times 3$$
$$411 \times 2$$
$$310 \times 1$$
$$212 \times 3$$

2
$$110 \times 7$$
$$141 \times 2$$
$$130 \times 3$$
$$302 \times 3$$

3
$$114 \times 2$$
$$524 \times 1$$
$$333 \times 3$$
$$230 \times 2$$

Zany and Brainy

Multiply.

1   314
   x 2
            230
           x 3

2   432
   x 3
            521
           x 4

3   604
   x 2
            702
           x 3

4   723
   x 3
      921
   x 2
      241
   x 2
      813
   x 3

5   112
   x 3
      124
   x 2
      303
   x 3
      620
   x 4

The school science lab has 3 sets of test tubes. Each set has 112 tubes. How many are there in all? Show your work on another sheet of paper.

Check It Out!

Multiply. Then, use a calculator to check your work.

1) 315
    x   9

2) 456
    x   4

3) 675
    x   5

4) 764
    x   7

5) 219
    x   8

6) 968
    x   3

7) 391
    x   4

8) 532
    x   6

9) 808
    x   4

10) 270
    x   9

 On another sheet of paper, write five multiplication problems with a three-digit number. Multiply. Check each answer with a calculator.

Number Fun With Barky

Write a number sentence for each problem. Solve.

---

1 Connor's dog, Barky, made 3 holes in the backyard. Connor's dad had to fill each hole with 78 scoops of dirt. How many scoops did his dad need in all?

2 Barky got into Steve's closet. He chewed up 8 pairs of shoes. How many shoes did he chew altogether?

---

3 Adrienne went to the store to buy doggie treats. She bought 6 boxes of doggie treats. Each box has 48 treats. How many treats in all did Adrienne buy?

4 Terri took Barky to the vet for 3 shots. Each shot cost $22.65. How much money did Terri pay the vet?

---

5 Max's job is to keep Barky's water bowl full. If he fills it 3 times a day for 24 days, how many times did he fill the bowl altogether?

6 Barky runs around the block 4 times every day. How many times does he run around the block in 5 days?

© Scholastic Inc.

Scholastic Success With Multiplication & Division • Grade 3   **25**

Tic-Tac-Toe

Multiply. If the ones digit in the product is less than five, mark an
O in the box. If the ones digit is five or greater, mark an **X**.
Are there three in a row?

Game 1

56 x 7	129 x 8	42 x 3
238 x 3	251 x 6	132 x 4
62 x 4	83 x 4	185 x 2

Game 2

97 x 3	189 x 4	224 x 4
76 x 4	55 x 8	252 x 3
225 x 4	304 x 2	58 x 3

 On another sheet of paper, make up your own multiplication tic-tac-toe game. Share your game with a friend.

Working With Area

Write a number sentence to find the area of each shape. Then, on another sheet of paper, write the multiplication and division fact families for each number sentence.

The **area** of an object is the number of square units needed to cover its surface. To find the area, multiply the length by the width. For example:
4 x 2 = 8 square units

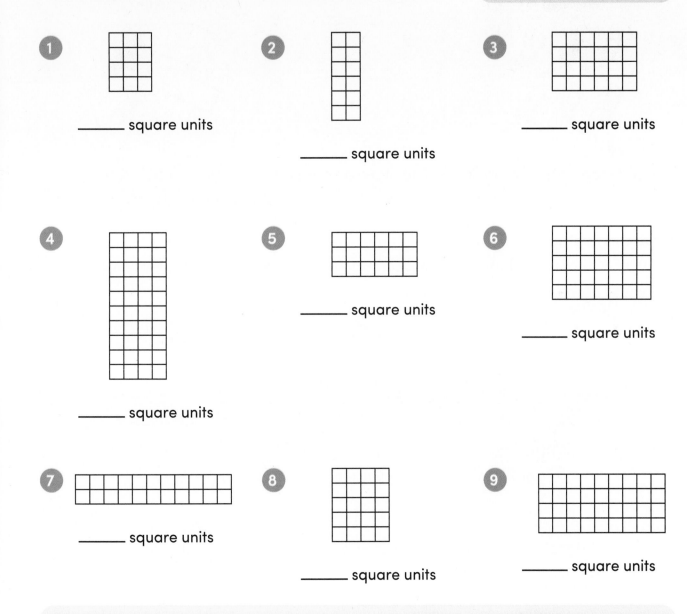

1 _____ square units

2 _____ square units

3 _____ square units

4 _____ square units

5 _____ square units

6 _____ square units

7 _____ square units

8 _____ square units

9 _____ square units

 The playground at school is 36 yards long and 9 yards wide. What is the area of the playground? On another sheet of paper, write an equation to find the answer.

What Is Division?

To **divide** means to make equal groups. The total number being divided is called the **dividend**. The number of groups the total is to be divided into is called the **divisor**. The answer is called the **quotient**.   6 ÷ 2 = 3

total number (dividend–6)	number of groups (divisor–2)	number in each group (quotient–3)

The pet store has 10 birds in all. The store owner wants to put the birds into the 5 new cages he bought. How many birds will he put in each cage?

Solve this problem by drawing a picture on another sheet of paper. Draw the number of birds you think need to go in each cage. (Hint: Each cage must have the same number of birds.) Then, complete the number sentence.

Total Number of Birds	Number of Cages	Number of Birds in Each Cage

_____ ÷ 5 = _____

What if the store owner only had 2 cages? How many birds would go in each cage? Draw a picture. Then, write a number sentence.

_____ ÷ _____ = _____

Filled With Marbles

Draw a circle around the correct number of marbles to show each division problem. Complete each number sentence.

1 8 ÷ 2 = __4__

2 6 ÷ 3 = _____

3 12 ÷ 3 = _____

4 10 ÷ 2 = _____

5 18 ÷ 3 = _____

6 9 ÷ 3 = _____

7 16 ÷ 2 = _____

8 15 ÷ 3 = _____

 On another sheet of paper, write a number sentence and draw a picture to show 12 marbles divided into 2 groups.

Alien Adventure

Divide.

1 6 ÷ 2 = ____   9 ÷ 3 = ____   10 ÷ 2 = ____

2 12 ÷ 3 = ____   14 ÷ 2 = ____   8 ÷ 2 = ____

3 2 ÷ 2 = ____   18 ÷ 3 = ____   24 ÷ 3 = ____

4 2)‾12‾   3)‾21‾

5 3)‾6‾   3)‾3‾

6 3)‾15‾   2)‾16‾

7 There are 18 aliens ready to board their spaceships. If 6 aliens get on each spaceship, how many spaceships do they need? Draw a picture on another sheet of paper to show the problem. Then, write a number sentence to solve the problem.

 On another sheet of paper, using the numbers 12 and 3, write your own word problem. Draw a picture and write a number sentence. Solve.

Flying Back

You can use a number line to help divide. Count back in equal groups to 0.
28 ÷ 4 = 7

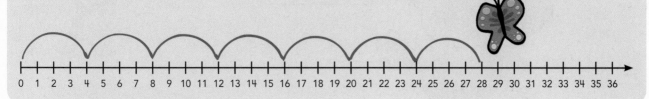

Divide. Use the number line to help you.

1 4)‾16‾   4)‾36‾   4)‾4‾   4)‾24‾

2 4)‾20‾   4)‾12‾   4)‾32‾   4)‾8‾

3 32 ÷ 4 = _____   16 ÷ 4 = _____   20 ÷ 4 = _____

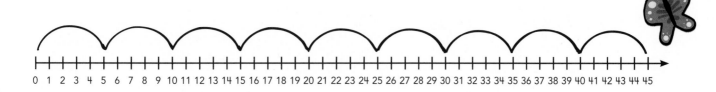

Divide. Use the number line to help you.

1 5)‾15‾   5)‾5‾   5)‾40‾   5)‾45‾

2 5)‾25‾   5)‾10‾   5)‾20‾   5)‾30‾

Dividing Is a Breeze

Divide.

① 30 ÷ 5 = _____   32 ÷ 4 = _____   45 ÷ 5 = _____   5 ÷ 5 = _____

② 36 ÷ 4 = _____   20 ÷ 4 = _____   25 ÷ 5 = _____   28 ÷ 4 = _____

③ 5)‾10‾   4)‾16‾   5)‾40‾   5)‾45‾   4)‾20‾

④ 4)‾12‾   5)‾35‾   4)‾8‾   5)‾15‾   4)‾24‾

⑤ Lisa tied a total of 12 ribbons on her kites. If she tied 4 ribbons on each kite,

how many kites does Lisa have? _____

 There were 36 people flying kites in the park. There were an equal
number of yellow, green, orange, and blue kites. How many kites were
there of each color? Show your work on another sheet of paper.

Dividing Evenly

Look at each number on the chart. Decide whether the number is divisible by 2, 3, 4, or 5. Circle each number using the color code. Some numbers will be circled more than once.

If a number can be evenly divided by a number, it is **divisible** by that number. For example: 2, 4, 6, 8, 10, and 12 are all divisible by 2. 3, 6, 9, 12, 15, and 18 are all divisible by 3.

Numbers Divisible by	Circle
2	red
3	orange
4	yellow
5	blue

4	7	9	21	15	22
25	28	40	18	30	5
31	32	11	14	3	35
2	27	12	36	16	20
8	6	24	29	10	45

 Choose two numbers you circled with three different colors. On another sheet of paper, write the three division number sentences for each number.

Leaping Lily Pads

Divide.

1 $6\overline{)30}$ $7\overline{)28}$ $6\overline{)12}$ $6\overline{)48}$

2 $7\overline{)49}$ $6\overline{)18}$ $7\overline{)35}$ $6\overline{)6}$

3 $21 \div 7 =$ _____ $7 \div 7 =$ _____ $42 \div 6 =$ _____

4 $14 \div 7 =$ _____ $24 \div 6 =$ _____ $36 \div 6 =$ _____

Divide by 6.

0	6	12	18	24	30	36	42	48	54

Divide by 7.

0	7	14	21	28	35	42	49	56	63

Field Trip Fun

Divide.

① 42 ÷ 7 = _____   54 ÷ 6 = _____   36 ÷ 6 = _____

② 24 ÷ 6 = _____   63 ÷ 7 = _____   48 ÷ 6 = _____

③ 14 ÷ 7 = _____   56 ÷ 7 = _____   28 ÷ 7 = _____

④ 49 ÷ 7 = _____   60 ÷ 6 = _____   42 ÷ 6 = _____

⑤ 56 students went on a field trip to an animal sanctuary. They traveled in 7 vans. How many students were in each van?

⑥ When the students went to where the monkeys lived in the sanctuary, they found it was divided into 6 areas. The same number of monkeys were in each area. There were 24 monkeys in all. How many monkeys were in each area?

 On another sheet of paper, add the quotients in each row of problems above. Which row has a sum equal to the total number of monkeys at the animal sanctuary?

The Skate Divide

Color each skate and helmet with the correct quotient.

$90 \div 9 = 10$

$8\overline{)72}$ → 9

$9\overline{)36}$ → 4

$56 \div 8 = 6$

$8\overline{)32}$ → 4

$24 \div 8 = 3$

$9\overline{)45}$ → 5

$48 \div 8 = 8$

$8\overline{)40}$ → 4

$9\overline{)18}$ → 2

$8\overline{)64}$ → 8

$63 \div 9 = 7$

$80 \div 8 = 11$

$81 \div 9 = 9$

On another sheet of paper, write the correct division number sentences for the problems above that you did not color.

Dividing Race

Use a stopwatch to time how long it takes to divide each runner's path to the finish line.

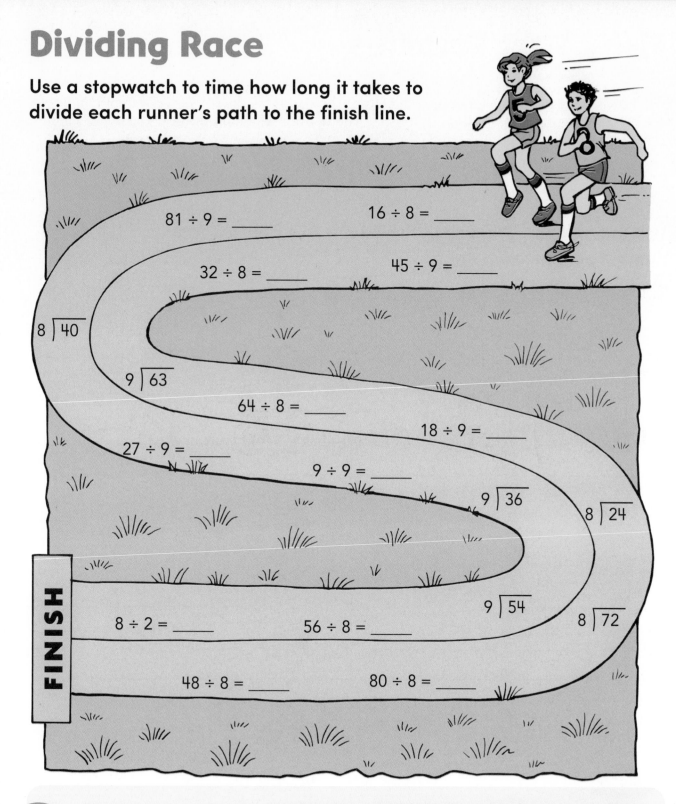

$81 \div 9 =$ _____

$16 \div 8 =$ _____

$32 \div 8 =$ _____

$45 \div 9 =$ _____

$8\overline{)40}$

$9\overline{)63}$

$64 \div 8 =$ _____

$18 \div 9 =$ _____

$27 \div 9 =$ _____

$9 \div 9 =$ _____

$9\overline{)36}$

$8\overline{)24}$

$9\overline{)54}$

$8\overline{)72}$

$8 \div 2 =$ _____

$56 \div 8 =$ _____

$48 \div 8 =$ _____

$80 \div 8 =$ _____

FINISH

Last week in track practice, Andy ran 36 miles. He ran the same number of miles on each of the 4 days. How many miles did he run each day? Show your work on another sheet of paper.

Fishy Fact Families

Division is the opposite of multiplication. The dividend, divisor, and quotient can be used to write multiplication sentences. The division and multiplication sentences are called a **fact family**.

15 ÷ 3 = 5 (15 divided into 3 equal groups)   3 x 5 = 15 (3 groups of 5)
15 ÷ 5 = 3 (15 divided into 5 equal groups)   5 x 3 = 15 (5 groups of 3)

Use the numbers from each fish family to write fact family number sentences.

1

_____ x _____ = _____

_____ x _____ = _____

_____ ÷ _____ = _____

_____ ÷ _____ = _____

2

_____ x _____ = _____

_____ x _____ = _____

_____ ÷ _____ = _____

_____ ÷ _____ = _____

3

_____ x _____ = _____

_____ x _____ = _____

_____ ÷ _____ = _____

_____ ÷ _____ = _____

4

_____ x _____ = _____

_____ x _____ = _____

_____ ÷ _____ = _____

_____ ÷ _____ = _____

5

_____ x _____ = _____

_____ x _____ = _____

_____ ÷ _____ = _____

_____ ÷ _____ = _____

6

_____ x _____ = _____

_____ x _____ = _____

_____ ÷ _____ = _____

_____ ÷ _____ = _____

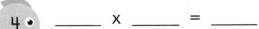

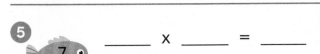

Over the Hurdles

Sometimes when you try to divide a number into equal groups, part of the number is left over. This is called the **remainder**. Use these steps to find the remainder.

1.

$$5{\overline{\smash{)}16}}$$

Think: 5 x ____ is the closest to 16.

2.

$$\begin{array}{r} 3 \\ 5{\overline{\smash{)}16}} \\ -15 \\ \hline 1 \end{array}$$

3.

$$\begin{array}{r} 3R1 \\ 5{\overline{\smash{)}16}} \\ -15 \\ \hline 1 \end{array}$$

There are 5 groups of 3 with 1 left over.

Divide.

1 $6{\overline{\smash{)}10}}$ $2{\overline{\smash{)}9}}$

2 $3{\overline{\smash{)}20}}$ $2{\overline{\smash{)}19}}$ $6{\overline{\smash{)}47}}$ $6{\overline{\smash{)}41}}$

3 $7{\overline{\smash{)}51}}$ $2{\overline{\smash{)}15}}$ $3{\overline{\smash{)}22}}$ $7{\overline{\smash{)}48}}$

4 $2{\overline{\smash{)}11}}$ $4{\overline{\smash{)}26}}$ $6{\overline{\smash{)}19}}$ $5{\overline{\smash{)}27}}$

More Remainders

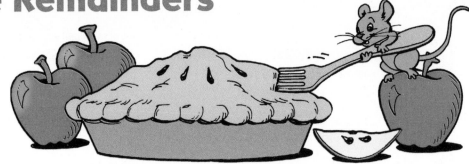

Divide.

1 5)‾41   6)‾52   3)‾19   8)‾74

2 4)‾29   2)‾13   7)‾38   9)‾46

3 5)‾21   6)‾31   3)‾26   8)‾57

4 4)‾14   2)‾7   7)‾65   9)‾51

5 3)‾13   6)‾39   5)‾14   8)‾50

 Candy's mom bought 56 apples to make 8 pies. If she used an equal number of apples in each pie, how many apples did she use in each pie? Solve on another sheet of paper.

Figure It Out

Divide. Answer each question.

1. A clothing store clerk has 14 sweaters. He wants to put them in equal stacks on 3 shelves. How many sweaters will be in each stack?

2. Mary needs to bake 71 cookies. Each cookie sheet holds 8 cookies. How many cookies are on the unfilled cookie sheet?

3. Luis is putting 74 cans into cartons. Each carton holds 8 cans. How many cans will be in the unfilled carton?

4. Rosa has 57¢. She wants to buy lollipops that cost 9¢ each. How many lollipops can she buy?

5. There are 17 cars waiting to be parked. There are an equal number of parking spots on 3 different levels. How many cars will not find a parking spot?

6. Don bought 85 crates of flowers. He separated them into groups of 9. How many equal groups did he have?

Keep on Dividing

Use these steps when dividing with greater dividends.

1. Divide the tens digit in the dividend by the divisor. Write the answer above the tens digit.

$$4\overline{)84}$$ with 2 above

2. Multiply the partial quotient by the divisor. Write the answer below the tens digit. Subtract. Bring down the ones digit.

$$\begin{array}{r} 2 \\ 4\overline{)84} \\ -8\downarrow \\ \hline 04 \end{array}$$

3. Divide the ones digit by the divisor. Write the answer above the ones digit. Multiply. Subtract.

$$\begin{array}{r} 21 \\ 4\overline{)84} \\ -8\downarrow \\ \hline 04 \\ -4 \\ \hline 0 \end{array}$$

Divide.

1 $3\overline{)66}$ $2\overline{)48}$ $3\overline{)93}$ $3\overline{)39}$

2 $3\overline{)96}$ $3\overline{)63}$ $2\overline{)68}$ $9\overline{)90}$

3 $3\overline{)99}$ $3\overline{)69}$ $2\overline{)80}$ $5\overline{)55}$

Dividing the Loot

Remember to follow each step when dividing larger numbers.

1. Divide the tens digit by the divisor. Multiply. Subtract.

```
     1
3 ) 45
   -3
    1
```

2. Bring down the ones digit. Divide this number by the divisor.

```
     1 5
3 ) 45
   -3↓
    15
```

3. Multiply. Subtract.

```
     1 5
3 ) 45
   -3↓
    15
   -15
     0
```

Divide.

1   2) 58   5) 85   6) 72   5) 90

2   3) 48   8) 96   2) 74   4) 92

3   6) 78   4) 76   5) 65   4) 60

Andrew has 87 marbles. He divides them into 3 bags. How many marbles are in each bag? Solve. Then, circle the problem above with the same quotient. Show your work on another sheet of paper.

It's All Relative

Remember that multiplication and division are related. Multiplying the quotient by the divisor will tell you the dividend.

Write each missing dividend.

1 ____ ÷ 9 = 7   ____ ÷ 4 = 6   ____ ÷ 6 = 6   ____ ÷ 5 = 7

2 ____ ÷ 3 = 3   ____ ÷ 2 = 9   ____ ÷ 8 = 6   ____ ÷ 9 = 9

3 ____ ÷ 4 = 8   ____ ÷ 3 = 7   ____ ÷ 2 = 8   ____ ÷ 6 = 3

4 ____ ÷ 8 = 8   ____ ÷ 1 = 9   ____ ÷ 5 = 6   ____ ÷ 7 = 1

5 ____ ÷ 4 = 40   ____ ÷ 3 = 30   ____ ÷ 3 = 100

6 ____ ÷ 7 = 60   ____ ÷ 5 = 60   ____ ÷ 2 = 40

Division Treats

candy cane
5¢

cookies
6¢ each

licorice
7¢

candy bar
9¢

jelly
beans
4¢

Write a number sentence for each problem. Solve.

1 Suzanne has 96¢. How many cookies can she buy?	**2** Connie has 84¢. How many cookies can she buy?
3 Lee has 98¢. How many candy bars can she buy? How much money will she have left over?	**4** Toby is in the mood for candy canes. How many can he buy with 63¢? How much money will he have left?
5 Jose has 72¢. How many jelly beans can he buy?	**6** Ann is buying licorice for her friends. How many pieces can she buy for 74¢? What could she buy with the remaining money?

Decision Time

Decide whether to
multiply or divide.
Solve.

---

1 Ellen baked 75 cookies in 3
hours. Joe baked 96 cookies in
4 hours. Who baked the most
cookies per hour?

2 James pitched 18 times in each
inning of the ball game. How
many times did he pitch in the
9 innings?

---

3 Lana bought 4 20-ounce sodas.
How many 4-ounce servings can
she give her party guests?

4 Cory's mom sent him to the store
for eggs. He bought 4 cartons of
a dozen eggs. How many eggs
did he purchase in all?

---

5 Maria made bracelets for her
friends. She put 9 beads on
each. She had 81 beads. How
many bracelets did she make?

6 It costs 50¢ per hour to park at
the beach. How much did it cost
David's parents to park for 8
hours?

ANSWER KEY

Page 5
1. 4, 9, 12 **2.** 12, 18, 21 **3.** 14, 18, 10
1. 2, 24, 10, 0, 6, 14 **2.** 8, 9, 3, 12, 0, 3

Page 6
Check students' arrays.
1. 12 **2.** 30 **3.** 10 **4.** 24 **5.** 32 **6.** 15

Page 7
B. 12 **R.** 4 **A.** 8 **F.** 32 **P.** 28 **S.** 30
U. 15 **E.** 5 **U.** 16 **I.** 25 **G.** 0 **S.** 10
O. 20 **D.** 45 **I.** 36 **N.** 24 **S.** 35 **C.** 40
SIRIUS and CANOPUS

Page 8
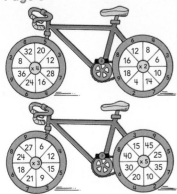

Extra Activity: 4 x 9 = 36 miles

Page 9
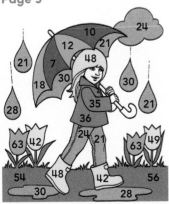

Check students' pictures.

Page 10
1. 36, 14 **2.** 7, 30 **3.** 12, 28
4. 0, 49 **5.** 42, 12, 63, 24, 36, 21
6. 18, 56, 6, 35, 54, 42
Extra Activity: 4 x 7 = 28 flowers

Page 11

Extra Activity: 8 x 2 = 16 cubs

Page 12
1. 54, 72, 40, 48 **2.** 27, 81, 56, 18 **3.** 72,
0, 16, 64, 54, 24 **4.** 36, 63, 9, 32, 0, 32
5. 27, 40, 63, 8, 45, 48

Page 13

Page 14

×	0	1	2	3	4	5	6	7	8	9
0	0	0	0	0	0	0	0	0	0	0
1	0	1	2	3	4	5	6	7	8	9
2	0	2	4	6	8	10	12	14	16	18
3	0	3	6	9	12	15	18	21	24	27
4	0	4	8	12	16	20	24	28	32	36
5	0	5	10	15	20	25	30	35	40	45
6	0	6	12	18	24	30	36	42	48	54
7	0	7	14	21	28	35	42	49	56	63
8	0	8	16	24	32	40	48	56	64	72
9	0	9	18	27	36	45	54	63	72	81

1. 3, 2, 9 **2.** 6, 6, 8 **3.** 9, 8, 2
4. 7, 9, 6 **5.** 5, 7, 8

Page 15
24, 32, 30, 42, 45
Extra Activity: 32 balls

Page 16
U. 46 **A.** 36 **Q.** 28 **E.** 93 **E.** 99 **J.** 213
D. 166 **!.** 88 **C.** 48 **N.** 55 **A.** 129 **S.** 148
R. 208 **S.** 66
SQUARE DANCERS!

Page 17
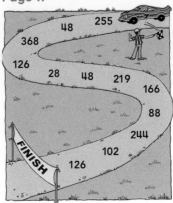

Extra Activity: 3 x 32 = 96 laps

Page 18
1. 144, 125, 441 **2.** 664, 432, 116, 282,
385 **3.** 310, 192, 290, 147, 384

Page 19
N. 204 **C.** 51 **A.** 184 **H.** 310 **I.** 318
B. 504 **S.** 112 **K.** 96 **R.** 108 **B.** 117
IN BRANCH BANKS!

Page 20
1. 159, 126, 184, 292 **2.** 204, 328, 175,
108 **3.** 150, 161, 156, 64 **4.** 58, 190,
288, 168
Extra Activity: Problems that did not
need regrouping: **1.** 53 x 3, 63 x 2
2. 82 x 4 **3.** 52 x 3, 32 x 2 **4.** 84 x 2
Pattern: 2 problems in row 1,
1 problem in row 2, 2 problems in
row 3, 1 problem in row 4

Page 21
1. 72¢ X 4 = $2.88 **2.** 29¢ X 6 = $1.74
3. 68¢ x 3 = $2.04 **4.** 87¢ x 3 = $2.61
5. 43¢ x 2 = $.86, 29¢ x 2 = 58¢,
86¢ + 58¢ = $1.44 **6.** 95¢ x 3 = $2.85,
68¢ x 2 = $1.36, $2.85 + $1.36 = $4.21

Page 22
1. 609, 822, 310, 636 **2.** 770, 282, 390,
906 **3.** 228, 524, 999, 460

Page 23
1. 628, 690 **2.** 1,296; 2,084 **3.** 1,208;
2,106 **4.** 2,169; 1,842; 482; 2,439
5. 336; 248; 909; 2,480
Extra Activity: 336 test tubes

Page 24
1. 2,835 **2.** 1,824 **3.** 3,375 **4.** 5,348
5. 1,752 **6.** 2,904 **7.** 1,564 **8.** 3,192
9. 3,232 **10.** 2,430

Page 25
1. 78 X 3 = 234 scoops of dirt
2. 8 x 2 = 16 shoes
3. 48 x 6 = 288 treats
4. $22.65 x 3 = $67.95
5. 24 x 3 = 72 times
6. 4 x 5 = 20 times

Page 26
Game 1:

392	1,032	126
O	O	X
714	1,506	528
O	X	X
248	332	370
X	O	O

Game 2:

291	756	896
O	X	X
304	440	756
O	O	X
900	608	174
O	X	O

Page 27
1. 4 x 3 = 12 **2.** 6 x 2 = 12 **3.** 4 x 6 = 24
4. 10 x 4 = 40 **5.** 3 x 6 = 18
6. 5 x 7 = 35 **7.** 2 x 11 = 22
8. 5 x 4 = 20 **9.** 4 x 9 = 36
Extra Activity: 36 x 9 = 324 square
yards

Page 28
Check students' drawings.
10 ÷ 5 = 2; 10 ÷ 2 = 5

Page 29
Check that students have circled the
appropriate number of marbles.
2. 2 **3.** 4 **4.** 5 **5.** 6 **6.** 3 **7.** 8 **8.** 5
Extra Activity: 12 ÷ 2 = 6

Page 30
1. 3, 3, 5 **2.** 4, 7, 4 **3.** 1, 6, 8 **4.** 6, 7
5. 2, 1 **6.** 5, 8 **7.** 18 ÷ 6 = 3 spaceships

Page 31
1. 4, 9, 1, 6 **2.** 5, 3, 8, 2 **3.** 8, 4, 5
1. 3, 1, 8, 9 **2.** 5, 2, 4, 6

Page 32
1. 6, 8, 9, 1 **2.** 9, 5, 5, 7 **3.** 2, 4, 8, 9, 5
4. 3, 7, 2, 3, 6 **5.** 12 ÷ 4 = 3 kites
Extra Activity: 36 ÷ 4 = 9 kites

Page 33
Check to see that students have
circled the numbers with the
appropriate colors.
Divisible by 2: 4, 22, 28, 40, 18, 30, 32,
14, 2, 12, 36, 16, 20, 8, 6, 24, 10;
Divisible by 3: 9, 21, 15, 18, 30, 3, 27, 12,
36, 6, 24, 45; **Divisible by 4:** 4, 28, 40,
32, 12, 36, 16, 20, 8, 24; **Divisible by 5:**
15, 25, 40, 30, 5, 35, 20, 10, 45

Page 34
1. 5, 4, 2, 8 **2.** 7, 3, 5, 1 **3.** 3, 1, 7
4. 2, 4, 6

0	6	12	18	24	30	36	42	48	54
0	1	2	3	4	5	6	7	8	9

0	7	14	21	28	35	42	49	56	63
0	1	2	3	4	5	6	7	8	9

Page 35
1. 6, 9, 6 **2.** 4, 9, 8 **3.** 2, 8, 4 **4.** 7, 10, 7
5. 56 ÷ 7 = 8 students
6. 24 ÷ 6 = 4 monkeys
Extra Activity: Row 4

Page 36

Extra Activity: 56 ÷ 8 = 7, 48 ÷ 8 = 6,
40 ÷ 8 = 5, 80 ÷ 8 = 10

Page 37

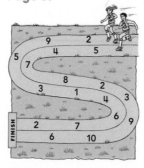

Extra Activity: 36 ÷ 4 = 9 miles

Page 38
1. 3 x 4 = 12, 4 x 3 = 12, 12 ÷ 3 = 4,
12 ÷ 4 = 3 **2.** 6 x 7 = 42, 7 x 6 = 42,
42 ÷ 6 = 7, 42 ÷ 7 = 6

3. 3 x 9 = 27, 9 x 3 = 27, 27 ÷ 3 = 9,
27 ÷ 9 = 3 **4.** 4 x 5 = 20, 5 x 4 = 20,
20 ÷ 4 = 5, 20 ÷ 5 = 4 **5.** 7 x 8 = 56,
8 x 7 = 56, 56 ÷ 7 = 8, 56 ÷ 8 = 7
6. 3 x 6 = 18, 6 x 3 = 18, 18 ÷ 3 = 6,
18 ÷ 6 = 3

Page 39
1. 1R4, 4R1 **2.** 6R2, 9R1, 7R5, 6R5
3. 7R2, 7R1, 7R1, 6R6
4. 5R1, 6R2, 3R1, 5R2

Page 40
1. 8R1, 8R4, 6R1, 9R2 **2.** 7R1, 6R1, 5R3,
5R1 **3.** 4R1, 5R1, 8R2, 7R1 **4.** 3R2, 3R1,
9R2, 5R6 **5.** 4R1, 6R3, 2R4, 6R2
Extra Activity: 56 ÷ 8 = 7 apples

Page 41
1. 14 ÷ 3 = 4R2, 4 sweaters
2. 71 ÷ 8 = 8R7, 7 cookies
3. 74 ÷ 8 = 9R2, 2 cans
4. 57 ÷ 9 = 6R3, 6 lollipops
5. 17 ÷ 3 = 5R2, 2 cars
6. 85 ÷ 9 = 9R4, 9 groups

Page 42
1. 22, 24, 31, 13 **2.** 32, 21, 34, 10
3. 33, 23, 40, 11

Page 43
1. 29, 17, 12, 18 **2.** 16, 12, 37, 23
3. 13, 19, 13, 15
Extra Activity: 87 ÷ 3 = 29 marbles

Page 44
1. 63, 24, 36, 35 **2.** 9, 18, 48, 81
3. 32, 21, 16, 18 **4.** 64, 9, 30, 7
5. 160, 90, 300 **6.** 420, 300, 80

Page 45
1. 96 ÷ 6 = 16 cookies
2. 84 ÷ 6 = 14 cookies
3. 98 ÷ 9 = 10 candy bars with
8 cents left over
4. 63 ÷ 5 = 12 candy bars with
3 cents left over
5. 72 ÷ 4 = 18 jellybeans
6. 74 ÷ 7 = 10 licorice pieces with
4 cents left over, one jelly bean

Page 46
1. 75 ÷ 3 = 25, 96 ÷ 4 = 24, Ellen
2. 18 x 9 = 162 times
3. 4 x 20 = 80, 80 ÷ 4 = 20 4-oz.
servings
4. 4 x 12 = 48 eggs
5. 81 ÷ 9 = 9 bracelets
6. $.50 x 8 = $4